Tricky TREE FROGS

by Natalie Lunis

Consultant: Dr. Kenneth L. Krysko
Senior Biological Scientist, Division of Herpetology
Florida Museum of Natural History, University of Florida

BEARPORT PUBLISHING

New York, New York

Credits

Cover and Title Page, © Michael Durham/Minden Pictures, Tororo Reaction/Shutterstock, and Videowokart/Shutterstock; TOC, © Sascha Burkard/Shutterstock; 4T, © Thomas Kitchin & Victoria Hurst/NHPA/Photoshot; 4B, © James Christensen/Foto Natura/Minden Pictures; 5, © Sebastian Duda/iStockphoto; 6T, © Marvin Dembinsky Photo Associates/Alamy; 6B, © Robert Valentic/Nature Picture Library; 7, © Dwight Kuhn/Dwight Kuhn Photography; 8T, © Custom Life Science Images/Alamy; 8B, © Andreas Huber/iStockphoto; 9T, © Nick Garbutt/Nature Picture Library; 9B, © David Kuhn/Dwight Kuhn Photography; 10, © Corbis/SuperStock; 11, © Fabio Liverani/Nature Picture Library; 12, © David Aubrey/Photo Researchers, Inc.; 13, © Michael & Patricia Fogden/Minden Pictures; 14, © Dwight Kuhn/Dwight Kuhn Photography; 15T, © Doug Wechsler; 15B, © Thomas Kitchin & Victoria Hurst/NHPA/Photoshot; 16T, © Dwight Kuhn/Dwight Kuhn Photography; 16B, © Juan Manuel Renjifo/Animals Animals Enterprises; 17TL, © Christian Ziegler/Minden Pictures; 17BL, © Christian Ziegler/Minden Pictures; 17R, © Premaphotos/Animals Animals Enterprises; 18, © Michael & Patricia Fogden/Minden Pictures; 19, © Dwight Kuhn/Dwight Kuhn Photography; 20, © Dwight Kuhn/Dwight Kuhn Photography; 21T, © Michael & Patricia Fogden/Corbis; 21B, © David Kuhn/Dwight Kuhn Photography; 22T, © George Grall/NGS Images; 22B, © Michael & Patricia Fogden/Minden Pictures.

Publisher: Kenn Goin
Editorial Director: Adam Siegel
Creative Director: Spencer Brinker
Design: Debrah Kaiser
Photo Researcher: Picture Perfect Professionals, LLC

Library of Congress Cataloging-in-Publication Data

Lunis, Natalie.
  Tricky tree frogs / by Natalie Lunis.
     p. cm. — (Amphibiana)
  Includes bibliographical references and index.
  ISBN-13: 978-1-936087-33-4 (library binding)
  ISBN-10: 1-936087-33-2 (library binding)
  1. Hylidae—Juvenile literature. I. Title.
  QL668.E24L864 2010
  597.87'8—dc22
                              2009042952

For more information, write to Bearport Publishing Company, Inc., 101 Fifth Avenue, Suite 6R, New York, New York 10003. Printed in the United States of America in North Mankato, Minnesota.

122009
090309CGD

10 9 8 7 6 5 4 3 2 1

Contents

A Flash of Color

High up in a tree, a red-eyed tree frog sits still on a leaf. Its legs are tucked in close to its body. Silently, a cat-eyed snake slithers along the same branch, flicking its tongue in and out. It has picked up the scent of the sleeping frog.

◀ A red-eyed tree frog asleep

The cat-eyed snake ▶ is one of many kinds of snakes that hunt red-eyed tree frogs.

Before the snake can move in for the kill, however, the little frog opens its big red eyes. It quickly stretches its body out and shows the bright blue and orange markings on its sides and feet. The flashes of color startle the snake, giving the frog a chance to leap to another tree—and to safety.

A red-eyed tree frog showing its colors

Sometimes a red-eyed tree frog's big red eyes are enough to startle an enemy long enough for the frog to get away.

A World of Frogs

People are often surprised to learn that some frogs live in trees. Yet about a third of the 4,000 **species** of frogs in the world are tree frogs. They live in bushes and tall grasses, as well as in trees. Where do all the other kinds of frogs live? Many live in water. The rest live on the ground, often digging holes to make safe underground homes.

◁ The green frog is a common frog that lives mostly in the water.

The striped ▷ burrowing frog lives on the ground.

Like all frogs, tree frogs belong to a large group of animals called **amphibians**. Most of the animals in this group begin their lives in water and then move onto land. Toads, salamanders, and newts are also amphibians.

◁ Like many frogs that live outside the water, the eastern gray tree frog depends on humidity in the air to keep its skin moist.

As adults, frogs and most other amphibians use body parts called **lungs** to breathe air. However, they also breathe through tiny holes in their moist skin. If an amphibian's skin dries out, it stops getting enough air and dies.

Surviving the Winter

Red-eyed tree frogs live mainly in the warm, wet forests of Central America. However, other kinds of tree frogs live all over the world. They can be found just about anywhere that plants and trees grow.

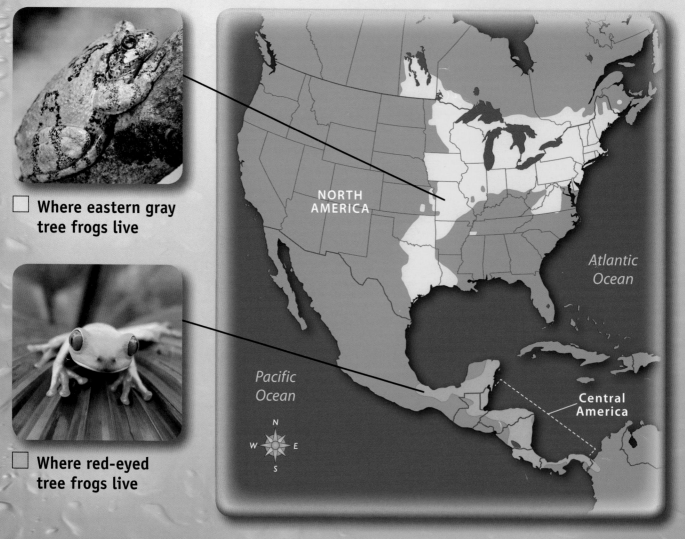

☐ **Where eastern gray tree frogs live**

☐ **Where red-eyed tree frogs live**

▲ Tree frogs live in most parts of the world. This map shows where two kinds—the red-eyed tree frog and the eastern gray tree frog—are found.

Many of the places where tree frogs make their homes have cold winters. For example, some eastern gray tree frogs live in parts of the northern United States and southern Canada. In places like these, tree frogs and other amphibians **hibernate**, or spend the winter in a deep sleep. They do so because their bodies cannot produce the heat they need to stay active.

The body temperature of frogs and all other amphibians rises or drops with the temperature of their surroundings. People call such animals **cold-blooded**. Scientists also use the word **ectothermic**.

⚠ **The rough-armed tree frog lives in forests in Asia that stay warm all year. Like the red-eyed tree frog, it does not need to hibernate.**

Eastern gray tree frogs and other hibernating tree frogs spend the cold winter months under logs, tree roots, or piles of leaves.

Finding Food

Like all amphibians, tree frogs are meat-eaters. They hunt mosquitoes, beetles, moths, and other insects in the plants and trees that they live in. Large sticky pads at the ends of the frogs' toes help them hang on as they climb from leaf to leaf and branch to branch.

Only tree frogs have feet with large sticky toe pads for climbing. Frogs that live in the water or on the ground have different kinds of feet.

toe pads

Tree frogs and other amphibians hunt only at night. The hot sun would dry out a tree frog's moist skin, so moving around and hunting after dark helps it survive.

A tree frog's big, **bulgy** eyes also help it catch food by allowing it to see all around. The eyes are especially good at spotting movement, so the frog is able to sneak up on insects as they fly, hop, or crawl nearby. As soon as the frog is close enough, it flicks out its tongue, which is long and sticky. Then it quickly swallows the insect.

Frogs swallow the insects that they catch whole, while they are still alive.

Tricking Enemies

Snakes, lizards, birds, and other animals hunt tree frogs in their leafy homes. The frogs have some surprising ways of staying safe from hungry enemies, however. The most important tricks they depend on have to do with color.

The color of a green tree frog's skin helps it stay hidden among leaves.

Some tree frogs, like the red-eyed tree frog, have colorful markings that can startle and confuse enemies. The main color of the frogs' bodies may be even more helpful, however. The red-eyed tree frog's bright green skin blends in almost perfectly with the leaves it sleeps on during the day. Other tree frogs have colors that look like tree bark. Their gray or brown skin lets them hide as they sleep on bark and woody branches.

Sleeping during the day helps keep tree frogs safe because they are even harder to see when they do not move at all.

△ **These gray tree frogs blend in perfectly with tree bark.**

Mating Calls

Pee-eep! Pee-eep! Pee-eep!

Tree frogs may be hard to see, but they are easy to hear. In many places, sounds like these fill the air in the spring. They are made by male tree frogs. Their calls help females find them so that the females can **mate** with them and lay eggs.

As a frog calls, a pocket of skin on its throat called a vocal sac fills up with air. This tree frog, called a spring peeper, is calling for a mate.

Every species of tree frog has it own call. The tree frog that repeats a loud "peep" is called the spring peeper. Another call that is well-known sounds like *quonk, quonk, quonk*. It comes from the green tree frog. Still another call is famous on the island of Puerto Rico. It sounds like *koh-kee, koh-kee, koh-kee*, and comes from a tree frog called the coqui (koh-KEE).

Like the spring peeper, the coqui was named for its call.

Many people think that most frogs have a call that sounds like *rib-bit, rib-bit, rib-bit*. In fact, however, only one kind of frog makes this sound. It is the Pacific tree frog, and it lives in California and other parts of western North America.

Pacific tree frog

Laying Eggs

Different tree frogs have different calls. They also lay eggs in different places and in different ways. Many kinds, including spring peepers, lay their eggs in the water, usually on plants or sticks.

A spring peeper laying eggs in a pond

Some kinds of tree frogs carry their eggs on their backs after laying them. Then, just after the babies hatch, the mother places them in a pond or stream.

Other kinds of tree frogs, including red-eyed tree frogs, lay their eggs on leaves above small ponds or puddles. As the eggs hatch, the baby frogs drop into the water below. Some kinds, such as African gray tree frogs, also lay their eggs above water, but they make a foam nest to protect them. When a heavy rain comes, it washes away the foam, allowing the eggs to drop into the water.

△ Red-eyed tree frog eggs

△ Red-eyed tree frog eggs about to drop into the water

△ The foam nest of an African gray tree frog

Hatching as Tadpoles

Baby tree frogs are called **tadpoles**. Their bodies are not at all like the bodies of adult tree frogs. They also live in a very different way.

△ **Red-eyed tree frog tadpoles**

Tadpoles are built for life in the water. They have body parts called **gills** that take in **oxygen** from water, just as fish do. They also have tails that they move back and forth in order to swim—but no legs. Instead of eating insects, they start out eating tiny plants and plant-like living things called **algae**.

A spring peeper tadpole

Like a fish, a tadpole is unable to breathe or survive outside the water.

From Water to Land

A few weeks after hatching, every tadpole starts to go through a big change. Scientists call what happens **metamorphosis**, which means "a change in form." The tadpole first grows back legs and then front legs. At the same time, its tail becomes shorter and shorter.

▲ **A spring peeper tadpole that has grown front and back legs**

Inside its body, lungs—which are used for breathing on land—grow as its gills start to disappear. Finally, after a few more weeks, the tadpole is a **froglet**. It climbs out of the water. Now a young tree frog, it is ready to live on land, hiding and hunting in plants, bushes, and trees.

A froglet has the body of a frog but with a short, stubby tail. In time, the tail disappears completely.

As fully grown adults, most tree frogs are only one to two inches (2.5 to 5 cm) long, and all are less than four inches (10 cm) long.

Spring peepers like this one grow to be about 1.5 inches (3.8 cm) long.

Tree Frogs in Danger

Tree frogs have been on Earth for millions of years. However, scientists fear that some species may now be in danger of becoming **extinct** due to diseases and changes in the **environment**.

Because tree frogs take in air and water through their skin, they are especially sensitive to **pollution**. Also, as more trees and forests are cut down, more tree frogs lose their homes.

In some places in the world, certain kinds of tree frogs are already extinct. Here are two kinds that are currently in danger.

Pine Barrens Tree Frog

- This tree frog is found in swamps in a large, sandy-soiled pine forest that stretches through 2,000 square miles (5,180 sq km) of New Jersey. It is also found in a few areas in North and South Carolina, Florida, and Alabama.
- Its call sounds like *quank, quank, quank*.
- The pine barrens tree frog is now threatened by the building of homes and businesses on the land where it lives.

Blue-sided Tree Frog

- This tree frog lives and hunts high in the trees of warm, wet forests in Costa Rica.
- Its call sounds like *wor-or-orp, wor-or-orp, wor-or-orp*.
- The blue-sided tree frog is in danger of disappearing because of pollution and the cutting down of forests. Also, like many kinds of tree frogs, these frogs are captured in the wild and then sold as pets.

Glossary

algae (AL-jee) tiny plant-like living things often found in lakes, ponds, and other bodies of water

amphibians (am-FIB-ee-uhnz) a large group of animals that usually spend part of their lives in water and part on land

bulgy (BUHL-jee) sticking out

cold-blooded (*kohld*-BLUHD-id) having a body temperature that rises and drops with the temperature of the environment

ectothermic (*ek*-toh-THER-mik) the scientific word for *cold-blooded*

environment (en-VYE-ruhn-muhnt) the area where an animal or plant lives, and all the things, such as weather, that affect that place

extinct (ek-STINGKT) when a kind of plant or animal has died out

froglet (FROG-let) a young frog that looks like an adult but is not yet fully grown

gills (GILZ) the body parts of a water animal that are used for breathing

hibernate (HYE-bur-nayt) to spend the winter in a deep sleep to escape the cold

lungs (LUHNGZ) the body parts of an animal used for breathing air

mate (MAYT) to come together to produce young

metamorphosis (*met*-uh-MOR-fuh-siss) the change that tree frogs and other amphibians go through from egg to adult

oxygen (OK-suh-juhn) a colorless gas that is found in the air and water, and that animals and people need to breathe

pollution (puh-LOO-shuhn) harmful materials that damage the air, water, and soil

species (SPEE-sheez) groups that animals are divided into, according to similar characteristics; members of the same species can have offspring together

tadpoles (TAD-*pohlz*) baby frogs

Index

Bibliography

Cassie, Brian. *National Audubon Society First Field Guide: Amphibians.* New York: Scholastic (1999).

Gilpin, Daniel. *Tree Frogs, Mud Puppies & Other Amphibians.* Minneapolis, MN: Compass Point Books (2006).

Hofrichter, Robert. *Amphibians: The World of Frogs, Toads, Salamanders, and Newts.* Buffalo, NY: Firefly Books (2000).

Read More

Kalman, Bobbie. *Tadpoles to Frogs.* New York: Crabtree (2009).

Netherton, John. *Red-Eyed Tree Frogs.* Minneapolis, MN: Lerner (2001).

Reda, Sheryl A. *Frogs and Other Amphibians.* Chicago: World Book (2005).

Learn More Online

To learn more about tree frogs, visit

www.bearportpublishing.com/Amphibiana

About the Author

Natalie Lunis has written many science and nature books for children. She lives in the Hudson River Valley, just north of New York City.